Scenes From Law School

Steve April

c/o POB 4475
Mountain View, CA 94040-0331

First Printing
ISBN 978-0-9744686-7-9

A Barberry Book

Also By Steve April

Poetry

Poet In California
The Unicorn And The Prom Queen
The Einstein Club
The Weavers
The Sunflower

Essays/Dialogue

Optimism, American Style

Contents

𝕾𝖈𝖊𝖓𝖊𝖘 𝕵𝖗𝖔𝖒 𝕷𝖆𝖜 𝕾𝖈𝖍𝖔𝖔𝖑

1

Perky Mary O., her father the judge, gave a speech
on our Moot Court day. I am wearing a tweed sports
jacket, white shirt, over long underwear. My case involves
welfare fraud. He gazes at me, then the other fellow, and
pronounces "DRAW."

2

Maria C., half Italian, half Japanese. Brilliant passion lady of
law school summer nights. We held hands and walked in Golden
Gate park. Her crazy uncle held a shotgun to her head, and
terrorized her as a little girl. He went batty in WW2. That was
the big one. No wonder she wanted to be a lawyer.

There was Ray, chef from Le Bistro, who fixed on law as a follow up career, "it's a cauldron" he'd say, burly thugmeister.

There was Paul from Walnut Creek, who wanted to be a real estate attorney, there was Kimberly, who wanted to do torts, bold and brassy, Paul earned a brown belt in tae kwon do.

There was Peter, from New Hampshire, who ridiculed our winter's temperate weather, who wanted to practice environmental law back east.

There was Sharon, a law school whiz, favorite of many professors, who would every so often throw up in the ladies room there. "Damn chick singer down the drain," she'd say, with tears in her eyes.

Our contracts professor, stoic Navy vet, skin like wrinkled parchment.

Our corporate law professor, who would reminisce "there I was in the Louisiana bayou, with the gators, inspecting rigs at dawn, wonderin' to myself, what the hell am I doing here?" rubbery, boyish charm.

What do the swaying boughs say in a summer breeze? I am
all ears.

Where are they now, these faces of yesteryear? Maria is a
patent attorney with a big name San Francisco firm. She got
hire by our patent professor, who was enamored with her.

Mary O. is an aide to a congresswoman. She is running
an election campaign.

We are the wall. We are the door.

My first law school party. Attractive young women in silk blouses
rustle by, gin in hand. Professors and students together. A
professor, John Richman, looks out the Hyatt window,
ten stories up, and says, "guys like me own this town."

Portrait Of The Lawyer As A Mute Lute

Mike, the private eye, comes into the office,
And goes to the fridge and pops a beer.
'He was into lots of stuff,' he tells Julie,
    the staff attorney,
'Gambling, girls, maybe drugs...'
'And now he's dead,' says Julie.
'Now he's dead,' Mike echoes.
'Any names for me?' 'Not yet, but I'm working
    on it.'
—'Because my guy says he was in Houston with his
    girlfriend
And they have a United ticket to prove it.'
'Hey, chill out, no problem,' says Mike. 'You're sitting
    pretty in the catbird seat.'
Mike flips his beer in the trash and pops another—
Flips Soul Asylum on the boombox and sings along,
'Runaway train on a one-way track,
Runaway train, never looking back.'
'Let Harris round up his usual suspects, slip me
    a C-note and I'll get back to you,' he offers
      and slides out of the room, smooth and low key,
        in his black trench coat.

Swan Island

1

Blond, towheaded children sell souvenirs,
Hang out at the lobster-station as we arrive on Swan Island,
Fishermen trawlers, white clapboards, blue sky,
We are walking past the cranberry bushes and lush deep-purple
    lilacs,
On the road to Bird Cove Harbor,
We are walking to a music festival with mixed emotions,
    cool breezy August night, winds rustling the treetops,
And the conifers are coning back and forth,
    genuflecting to the aspens and the oaks are meditating
      in calm repose,
No Mapplethorpes here, just the pristine protected American
    heartland, green coasting summer,
One father and son team joking around, sharing a hot dog,
    dad with t-shirt that invites 'hear me, feel me,
      touch me, heal me.'
Tourist couples nibble on crab meat.
And the ospreys are restless and the sun is glinting
    off the juniper berries,
Go osprey go, gliding into the smooth summer sunsets,
Nothing better that the smooth silhouette of an osprey
    traversing the telephone wires and golden pastures,
Vistas of lakes surrounded by jackpines and genuflecting
    conifers.

2

An elderly couple in their backyard look out mesmerized by the
　　　　pristine vistas,
American flags fluttering proudly over windswept pine needles
　　　　and rusty TV antennae.

> *"full fathom five thy father lies*
> *those are pearls that were his eyes*
> *of his bones are coral made,*
> *nothing of him that doth fade*
> *but does suffer a sea-change*
> *into something rich and strange—*
> *sea-nymphs hourly ring his knell*
> *ding-dong, ding-dong bell..."*

O send me your buoys, your tall ships, send me your
　　　　savior searchlights
Or I will see sea nymphs surfacing over the golden marlins,
　　　　sea nymphs riding bareback on the darting marlins,
Darting in and out of the slithering skiffs,
We are all creatures of habit and that is why we are
　　　　addicted to the bells of rhyming searchlights,
Even the man with the sunburned hands who walked on roads
　　　　to Timbuktu amid the silver pinions dropping
　　　　like chains from Diana's chariot,
Like silver chains drawing him to her dim mysteries
　　　　the goddess alone consecrates...

3

Sounds of camaraderie reverberating to dawn's early light,
Families together in their sleeping bags, extended, reciprocal,
In their nature love fest,
The steep hills we all walked tonight,
The twelve life jackets in front of me...
Dim murmuring voices of fellow passengers
Or victims of blood-lust under a dim sad moon,
A Big Dipper bright and sparkling
Tosses a shooting star...
Eavesdropping on the philosophy of the fat man aboard the
    S.S. *Victory Chimes,*
Intelligent people intimating absolutely nothing.
A girl as fair-skinned as the underbelly of a dolphin.
My hands are sunburned, my body taut as a wavering leopard,
Taut and tender surveying the rolling hills of Swan Island,
Wonder why they call it Swan Island? No swans to be seen.
Were there once swans abdicated by cruel tyrants?
Nothing more peaceful than calm boats at harbor
    and lovely lullabies of ding-dong bells.
O dad, your picture comes to me.
A few images, pulled from the waters of the darkening
    mind.
Our host, our body's bread, dad.
—"We're going to be moving soon," you stoic to your
    six-year-old, then off to Delaware,
The way you said a prayer at evening meal, solemn

but relaxed,
The Navy ships you herded your three young children to,
the war fresh in your mind, on weekends in Delaware,
how you served in the Navy after the war, and learned
about radars and rubbers.
On other weekends, your kids like birds on a wire, listening
to *The Mikado*, or *The Pirates of Penzance*, or Mozart.
(You made us sit there. Hated that stuff then, like it now.
Hmm, what would you think, Bach my favorite?)
Once listening to Mozart's *Don Giovanni*, big father Imago,
you turned and said, "is that how you think of me?"
Visiting your workplace as a kid, florescent IBM warehouse,
your co-worker saying, "he'll be bald, like his father."
Later visiting you at Amdahl, cramped little office, nice salary,
your exhaustion in the evenings.
You would listen to Mozart, face pointed to the ceiling,
until nodding off.
—Rational computer engineer, needing music so badly.
You often seemed a Dr. Know (or No), your favorite moniker,
with sly humor,
But civilization and technology, part of a great Yes,
The march onward, as Rimbaud says,
Though with the smoke of battle in our nostrils, blood
on our lips, but oh so corporate.
You used to joke that universities were pettier than industry,
"no rest for the idle," or some such.
You did not care to treat your diabetes—looking for a better place
or simply tired out?
"See you in heaven," I said as you died.

4

Captain Kip Files, commander of the *S. S. Victory Chimes*,
        proud three-masted windjammer that sails the coast
        of Maine March to September
Gave us leave to go on shore, no sallow whiskerado he.
We will remember the stag bursting from the underbrush
As stars swarmed over Swan Island,
A night that seemed pregnant with golden ospreys,
        Shakespeare, dad.

The Seed

In grassy dusk, hands twined like lover trees in myths,
    I am as one green blade. Another evening
O luminous eyeball sun, another murk o blazey trip seed
    through the sky who trembles
Dew-eyed into luminous earth thrones,
Dew-eyed into lode of passion graves, magnetic flourishings,
    mighty insistent flames under the hill.

Courage, you who are a boy with red hair eternally whistling
    airy message notes like germs on dreamy lake.

Red Rose

On a little day like today you were born
     torn from the same feminine womb,
    held in the same feminine arms,
      while the crowds walked around outside
       doing their tasks.
Water streamed oblivious to your presence
    no rocks got up to sing,
    the sheep and the shepherds were
     out in the meadow, as usual.
   Child of Woman when did you first see
    the Earth was a Paradise?
     when did the sky give off
      that first intense ray of too-golden
       clarity,
     making you think of Eternity Here and Now?
   when did the birds and the animals in the valley
    grow those luminous rings around their heads
     showing you they were creatures of the
      One Universe?

"The kingdom of Heaven is in your heart,"

you said.
For 2,000 years after
    men have defiled
        screaming, scheming, clawing, sobbing,
           raising swords to place in other people's breasts
        mad with it, trying to make it
          into your Heaven...
Ah! How many were using you, your shining
        face and sexy body,
        they needed you for a symbol
          to explain their Madness away.
Are you smiling at the way
        they misused you, your comings
          and goings a thing they could not understand
          or penetrate, just walking
          around with a different look in your eye
        which made them stop and think for a second
        who is this guy?
You floated up from the Unconscious
        Breast of the Universe, your eyes a little warmer,
          to raise the temperature of Humanity for a time,
        your ways a little stranger, to make us pause
          in the midst of our machine.
        Eternity dazzled your eyes
          until you dreamed everything was dazzling.
When they stuck a sword in your side
        and your blood flowed, it flowed golden
          —only one moment when the Vision failed!

Now the winter is upon us,
    we break bread and almost never think of you
      this day, you a flower
        blooming in the minds of our best moments.
You saw slender Eternity
    bow and grace the earth with a kiss
    before the wintertime of spears, deceptions,
      snowed down on you like snowflakes
        and broke your summer heart...

We Are Recorders!

O chaos of art and science dripping with the blood of pioneers;
O chain of thanks and sacrifice perfectly formed;
We, in our strength, in our weakness, form your badge, our wound,
We come to you on our knees...

Almost A Rainbow

Away from these shoals, shallows and sandbanks,
Multilingual languid mermaids,
Easy, generous and warm,
Their giggles, guffaws,
Their chortles, chuckles,
Sound of laughter near the
      islands.
To these I journey
The sky above almost a rainbow.

The Golden Gate

1

Another beautiful day, amid the drought.

May 27, 1937 the bridge opens, 200,000 walkers
    marvel at the 4,200 foot long span,
        connecting San Francisco and Marin County, CA.
The next day opens to vehicles.
Proposed in 1872, but not taken seriously until
    the 1920s,
Morrow along with his wife Gertrude develop
    the Golden Gate "art deco" design, choosing
        the color "international orange" to
            fit the Golden Gate moniker like a glove,
Aid visibility in the fog, and give the people
    something to gawk about.
Vermillion volley that resists rust and fading,
The '5' tall Cincinnati main engineer Strauss smiles,
    in parade, among the rufous.

2

Construction begins in 1933, in the depths of the
    Great Depression,
Blasting 65 feet below the water to plant
    earthquake-proof foundations,

Dealing with rogues tides, outrageous storms, and
     ubiquitous fog, at 4,200 feet the longest bridge
          in the world,
Counties north took out a large bond, Marin, Sonoma, Del Norte,
     Mendicino, paid back through bridge toll,
Homes, farms, businesses, put up as collateral to build the bridge.
(May 21, 1937 Amelia Earhart flew over the
     completed structure, before meeting her mysterious
          end near tiny Howland Island, in the Pacific.)

3

Over 550,000 rivets in each tower,
In four years it was done.
Steel loaded in sections onto railroad cars,
     in Trenton, Sparrows Point, Bethlehem,
          Pottstown, and Steelton,
Shipped through the Panama Canal to San Francisco.
On Feb 17, 1937 10 men lost their lives, when
     a section of scaffolding collapses, and they
          miss the safety net.
The "Halfway To Hell" club remembers, safety net
     suspended during construction under the
          floor of the bridge saved these 19 men.

4

The Golden Gate strait, the entrance to the San Francisco
    Bay, from the Pacific Ocean, named by
        Army Captain John Fremont, in 1846.
Commuters, so recently nude, on way to work, etude,
Lift their ardors, azure interludes.

When In Rome (A Satire)

Linger at the elbow joint with light, circular motions you use
        at the knee,
Allow your tongue to be moist, saliva is a fine lubricant,
Be an explorer, try deep suction in the vulnerable area
        below his ribs,
Open your mouth wide.
Your goal is not to cause pain but bring about a healing,
Move slowly as though your hair were fingers,
Let your hair do the caressing, avoid his face,
Using the balls of your fingers.

The Weaver And The Shepherd

1

Past moored ships in his seaport town
A merchant goes walking, bare head cast down,
Tears fly from his eyes, pulling his hair,
His ship crashed on rocks beyond repair
Lost, all lost, in tempests wild
His wife at home, pregnant with child
Until from the white foam that flies
He hears a voice, "merchant, your cries
Are plaguing my tides, they too cry out,
For their sake and yours, here is a way out.
If you will give me one thing I lack
Riches I promise to give you back.
Give me the youngest thing in your house,"
And the merchant stood, quiet as a mouse
Observing her silky hair, oval face
Green eyes, fresh smile, tail primly in place,
Thinking, "a greyhound pup, you're welcome to that,"
So he gave his promise and doffed his hat.
The mermaid kept her part of the bargain,
Proud ships came in, with riches laden.
But then to realize wife bore his son
Only hours before the promise he'd given!

"Never will Swenson visit the shore,"
Day after boy's birth, his father swore.
The land-locked lad hunted with skill
And became an expert in arts of the kill,
Volunteering for good king's hunt brigade
And gained fame for courage in the glade.
Off at dawn with the pack of yelping hounds
And king's horsemen as the horn sounds,
Corner wolf in the brake, then aims the king
Piercing arrow to flank as wild dogs sing.
Or king might order him garland a rump
While dogs trained for jugular rally and jump,
And harry the poor beast with mouths that foam
Sharp teeth, hungry bites, and howl until home.
So pleased was king with this dashing lad
He offered his daughter, and she was glad
As she loved Swenson, his dashing commands,
His boldness and vigor, the strength in his hands,
Fair contrast to business at the king's court,
Flattering couriers, and their perfumed sport.

3

Early one morning on fields of gold
A brown spotted hare sprints from the fold,

And startles his mare so he gives chase
As it bounds for brush in a panic haste,
And takes him winding and weaving toward
Where mermaid waters to claim her reward.
She throws a great wave at water's edge
And drags him down under to her coral ledge.
Her servants bind him with silver chains
As she swims forward and explains,
"Now you are mine and will do what I say,
You will learn to love the mermaid way."
"You are a lovely mermaid, but never by force
Will you win my love or change its course,
As my love is sworn to a lady true,
And bonded too sweetly to trade her for you!"
Next day mermaid, her love to attract
Comes bearing flowers and softer attack,
And clings to his neck, with tears imploring
Singing his praises, in tones adoring,
Urging him forgo trembling and fearing,
For her immortality, with words endearing
Saying, "here with me, riches are abounding,
Jewels plentiful and blue whales sounding
In harmony with our mother sea,
Touch the fountainhead, by touching me."

Meanwhile the princess, mild and good,
Dreams of a kind lady, and cottage in wood,
Who comforts her with the following words,
"As your love is true as the fields and birds,
Hear what I say—mermaids like pretty things
Go down to the shore, where the wild waves sing
And bring a gold comb, prince is her vassal
—When she claims the comb, grab hold and wrestle
The prince from her watery hold
—Prepare to struggle, you must be bold."
That night by a shore far from town
Along the dunes comes princess and lays comb down,
There touches her prince, his face in the waves,
As comb disappears, with her lover grave.
"Oh lady from dreams, please tell me how
To win back my prince, what shall I do now?"
Again this same lady appears in her dream
With kind face by a silver stream,
Saying, "take a flute down to shore and play.
The mermaid will want to take it away,
As she loves music and pretty baubles,
In the wave is your promised, reach for your double."
Next night princess returns to shore
Long flowing hair, white dress as before,
Playing soulful and sweet to queen moon above,
Sad plaint about her captured love.

Mermaid throws wave to gather in flute
—Prince touches her hand—poor substitute—
Again Princess weeps full of sadness and fears
The kind old lady, comforting and dear
Urges, "each time he's closer, take courage and steel
Yourself for tomorrow, bring a spinning wheel."
Next evening struggling over rock and sand
Comes princess spinning wheel in hand.
His thread in her loom, she grabs his neck,
And leaps in his arms as waves gather him back.
"If I can't have him, either will you,"
Shrilly cries mermaid and changes the two
—Prince turns into mackerel, silver and slick,
And princess to herring, shapely and thick,
As memory fades, tossed wide in fierce storms,
Until each touch shore and return to form.

5

He is a shepherd tending his flocks,
She is a weaver, shearing their locks.
Quiet hands, wan smile, and sad eyes confess
A hidden grief, a weaver's distress.

Something deep stirs within him as she lays
Thread on the loom—a scene from old days—
"What do you weave?," he inquires in amaze,
As his sheep graze on the pastures of praise.
"Dazed and confused, now I remember,
A crazy mermaid, you saved me from her."
With depth-dark sobs and laughs they embrace
By her loom, and gaze face to face,
Return to their kingdom, older and wiser,
And adopt three sons, Dave, Otto, and Kaiser.

The Mermaid In Town

1

A youthful mermaid plays with her seals,
Frolics by coral with walrus and eels,
Her most dear possession by far, and her wealth
Entrusted by her mother to keep in good health
She raises up from babies, their pretty guide
And oh how she treasures their company beside,
A small herd under the mermaid Lil,
Some sea-grey cows and a big bull named Bill.
One day grazing under the waves
They gently voice concerns, saying 'save
The seaweedy trash for fish, dear, we need
Quality food, on grass we should feed.'
There, close to shore, lay a fresh stretch of grass
Enthroned like a queen on her bull, they pass
From the waters to the sandy beach
And she says, 'my dears, your grass is in reach.'
Beyond stretch of grass in a little town
On Main Street rumors swirl up and down
On a hot summer day, invaders have come,
To terrify children and wreck happy homes.

2

'I have an idea,' connives the lawyer,
'We'll make her pay damages, this pretty destroyer,
Well known, they have riches under the sea
Her pearls and rubies is a proper fee.'
'Yes,' the crowd cheers, 'make her taxes heavy,
For eating our grass is our right to levy.'
'But I have no money,' mermaid exclaims,
'Just this girdle of rubies and pearls to my name,'
Says the lawyer, 'you make our hearts melt,
If you value your freedom, give up your belt.'
The mermaid's belt glistens with jewels bright
Her sea treasures gathered in hours of delight
They thought, 'we'll take them to city and sell,
And be millionaires, hard days farewell.'
Advises the lawyer, 'leave your girdle and go
Saucy wench, and retrieve from below
Two more girdles and in three days return,
Enough idle threats,' —so the mermaid turns
Amid their jeers and sadly departs
On top of her bull, with a troubled heart.

3

Lawyer says, 'for the city I will prepare,
Give me the jewels, I'll write you from there.'
'Are you high,' says the mayor, 'on loco weed?
The butcher and tailor are what you need.'

'Money talks so they say,' opines the pettifogger.
'My office will glitter and be full of joggers
Who say, 'alas, is a nasty divorce,
Deluge my husband with legal costs.'
'When I'm rich I'll buy horses for racing,
Instead of chopping I'll train them for pacing,
Smoke cigars when I win,' brags the big butcher,
'Have plenty of babes and plenty of culture.'
'I'll have the money to make wise decisions,'
Confides the tailor, 'the main thing is vision.
New polyesters are coming down the pike,
Teenagers are key, find out what they like.'
So each, as it were, with a big smile,
Eagerly makes plans for their change in life-style.
Halfway to city they pause by milestone
To ease aching legs and rest their bones,
Each dreaming of riches face to face,
They peek at the girdle, lifting the lace.
Great rubies and pearls shine in the sun,
And well-cut diamonds in pretty runs.
'Why waste time in the dust here and tarry?
Let's go,' says the butcher, 'my turn to carry.'
The lawyer grabs one part, butcher the other,
Amid pleas from tailor, they wrestle each other,
And the precious jewels scatter up and down,
Turn to dried seaweed, withered and brown.

Three nights later by the walls of the town,
Lawyer and butcher lay her seaweed down.
'More girdles?' asks the mermaid, 'more diamonds for free?'
And laughing she dives back in the sea.

The Curious Mermaid

While other mermaids swim debonair
Under the sea and comb their gold hair
A curious mermaid, Misty, was frisky,
And tends to regions her elders deem risky.
'Stay away from humans, not even a glance,
They will break your heart if given a chance,'
Confides a seahorse, 'the sea is your home,
We need you here in the white wave and foam.'
After a hard day's plowing his wheat and oats
Or baling hay, he goes down to his boat
And drifts in the cooling waters to find
Where the fish jump and he can unwind.
In the gray twilight he flings out his line
Whistling to the breeze as a new moon shines,
When he feels his line tug and reels in
What seems like a sprite who slips off again.
When she meets her friend, the whale, she says
'Tell me of humans, are they so bad?'
'Some are evil our elders agree,
Are afflicted with ills—or insanity,
Little one, stay by us, we have dear arms,
They will laugh at your tail or make fun of your charms.'
'But the farmer is so handsome, his arms are so strong,
I can't help myself, can my heart be wrong?

Does the moon glow? Does sun rise in the east?
Do I hold feet against him, not in the least!'

2

'Their arrival puts us in a pretty fix
They take more and more when we mix,'
Confides a passing dolphin, 'even our waves
They imagine they own, as if we were slaves.'
Still when the shadow of his boat passes over
The lovelorn Misty shoots up in the water,
Breaks surface to gaze at the farmer above,
And cries loud, 'oh,' struck speechless with love.
Young farmer, fishing line hanging from stern
Surprised as could be, gazes back in turn
Her long golden hair dazzles her shoulders,
But his blue eyes look at her colder.
Later, she dawdles, dreaming of him,
And perches on a rock next day after swim
And combs down her hair, golden and long
And serenades fishes with sweetest love songs.
But the young farmer is hard and conceited,
He thinks her beastly, her songs are too heated,
So in time her love ballads turn to wailing
And the farmer laughs and goes on sailing.
Then the mermaid carries gifts and love notes
Dumps emeralds, rubies into his boat,
But the farmer throws them back in the sea

And calls out, 'keep your garbage away from me.'
And the gulls clap their wings and shout, 'wa wa wa,'
Later, on land, as he drives his plow.

3

But Misty loves her farmer too much,
Guides him to best fishing grounds with her touch.
'Well you're some use after all,' he teases,
So she feels bolder, the more she pleases,
'I love you, I love you, give me a kiss,'
And climbs in his boat, 'oh no pretty miss.'
And angry he tosses her back in the sea,
'How can I love you, you're a big fish to me.'
And with that finally Misty gets mad
Sends big waves to swamp the mean spirited cad,
But how can he fight what turns into bog?
He limps back to land in a storm and a fog.
Next day he seeks counsel from Widow Crouch
Speaks to her of comb, mirror and pouch,
'Get a hold of her belt, she'll be wax in your hands,
The belt holds her strength, you understand.
If you wonder how, here is a ruse,
Oh this is cruel, the trick we will use,
Pretend and deceive her, kiss her lips,
Go fishing with her, praise her back flips,
Play the young fool—oh be her best friend,
Til she puts her belt in your hands.'

So he went off, and did as she said,
And after some days playing tricks with her head
'Ha ha, I'm master, don't argue or scold,
I have your belt, do as your told,
One day I'll release you but until then
You'll be my slave and sleep in the pigpen.'

4

Straw in her hair she begs for comb and mirror,
Day after day he laughs and refuses her.
Day after day she grows untidy, tangled,
Dispirited, disheveled, floppy and mangled.
Dogs snap at her when she draws near
This sad lonely mermaid in alien pastures,
A very Ruth, amid fields and sparkling sun,
Exiled from her water, her belt all undone.
Her cruel keeper would go fishing at dusk
Lock her in the pigpen and feed her corn husks,
Or invite his neighbors over for a date,
And mock and taunt her and her helpless state.
One evening the boy who herds his geese,
A towheaded lad with quick smile and bow knees
Curious about her asks, 'why do you cry?'
'Because I'm a mess,' she says, 'woe am I.'
'Please excuse my master, he works very hard,
And I am sad that this farm is your prison yard,
He yells at me if I'm slow at chores,
And docks me my dinner, as he docks you yours.'

'Without my comb I can't do my hair,
Without my belt, can't get back to my lair,
Be a good boy and go fetch my belt'—
Which he carries to her and oh how she felt!

5

She rises on her tail and does a back flip,
Combs the straw from her hair and her tail-tip,
Rides a horse to the sea and turns back,
And throws him a purse that lands on a haystack.
She sings with the sea, she sparkles near shore,
'For you, all for you, my sweet boy—and more.'
Oh what a rage when the farmer comes home,
His slave somehow fled, with her belt and comb.
This arrogant landlord rushes to the water,
Up rolls a huge wave, and tumbles him under,
Is all he can do, wrestling the riptide,
To drift back alive, while sea creatures chide.
And each year when the harvest moon shines
A towheaded lad walks the shoreline,
And follows her singing, 'for my hero bold,'
And finds on shore a purse filled with gold.

The Armored Archer

After 2,200 years
He scans the slate-colored room
For the enemies of
    Qin Shi Huang,
China's first emperor.
In those days they buried the horses
    and warriors
With the king.

Lawyer

for Sherman K.

After I won a little jackpot in Vegas
A guy sauntered over and asked 'are you Irish?'
They offered me a t-shirt or a photo
And I said, 'you don't know my friends,
I need a photo…' Too pure, too sensitive,
My hardboiled friends would mock and jibe,
Because I swooned in a Hall of Justice elevator,
Or because I retched in the men's room
During a break, as I helped defend a killer.

Forty Years Old

The child chasing a bird continued her chase,
Roller girl skating by the river continued her skate,
The pleasure cruises proceeded by unfinished skyscrapers
    to the Statue of Liberty,
And the clocks did not rewind to zero.

After 40 years he awoke from his dream,
A flaming savior with memories of whips and chains,
The pristine brilliance of azure and his childhood forever
    entwined
As the mountain and valley crumpled from a volcano,
    then rose again.

Clouds

Vulnerable as the tender heart
Of a young girl not yet become a wife
They laze along the open days' perfection over the treetops.

They gaze down, an eye through airy dreams, do nothing
But lift our eyes to the image of their flight,
Our aspirations like Daedalus, likewise our solitude.

This is what the sky is for, this is
How the heart of man must meet the sky, accept
The anguish of sensitive distant fires in his skin

Which yet do always rise above him, everlasting
Past his life, engaging creation in its colors, serving
To remind us of this love.

Darkling

In the evening when the trees
Break their leaves against the stars
The lonely lot of breathing
Breaks a warm chord from afar...

The lonely lot of being
Breaks its one chord from afar
—Drifts through any open window
To tell us who we are.

Door, window, breathing,
Opens out into the far
Distance, and our silence
Tunes the air to who we are.

And the music of our breathing
Can be heard, too, from afar,
And the sound of voices, falling
Through a rumor full of stars.

Fluorescence

There is a certain look that grows not in the field,
Nor stipples fragrant landscapes, mongered blue with sun;
Nor inklings the brute charity of air, nor ever yields
Warm image to the mind of anyone;

It is a look that sheds no rash of light
Upon the winded consciousness of the unfathomed seed,
Conjures no phalanx of corporeal brood to fight
In iron pauses disrupts every Them that breeds;

I have seen this look upon my woeful door;
Felt closing casements barrel me to harm;
Felt like a deer in flight on the forest floor
Every nerve on edge, in dire alarm;

The poxy of its input lockjaws breath;
Causes life to shuttle Lethe-wards abstract death.

United

Nor the miles that compose this winding journey
Nor the wide open expanses sailing by,
Nor the current, always present sun,
Nor the curving road down the danger mountain,
Nor the familiar road that leads to your house
Takes the hurt away tonight,
But the big cat rubbing my feet, the note on the table,
Helped me claim my estate among colossal powers
For a moment united me, myself, and I,
And the porcelain Buddha on the mirror smiling
Behind the candle shared the joke.

White Dog

The white dog chasing pine cones in the summer sun
At my friend's house
And suddenly I was back, back,
Looking for my friend, Myrna, who had not
Come home from school.
I was six or seven, and when her mother
Called our house to say she had run away,
My brother and I went looking for her.
We found her by the edge of the lake,
Dangling her feet. She had her big white dog,
Chubby, with her, and after we took her home
Her mother gave her a good talking-to, but let her
Wear a special little necklace,
And we had milk and cookies.
When our family moved a year later
I never saw her again, but I remember how she was drawn
To that lake where
Her sister had drowned the year before.

The Good Buddhist

I rise from the booth in the diner
And saunter over to the counter and the pies,
    deciding between lemon meringue,
      double cheesecake, German chocolate,
      backed by mirrors,
And walk back with my selection
    under the red Exit sign
      to where Bill is waiting,
    past the couples fondling
      and toddlers playing on the floor
—A good Buddhist observes this
    as a series of masks, illusions
—Even the 'I' that acts
    is a mask, Bill would say
—To learn to live with contradictions
    is a spirit path.
—And without these masks
    who are we?

Fireworks

Tonight is about unformed youth—
    Their departure for an armed truth
        To show their might and strength.
Eager to show how they can handle
    Each cherry bomb and Roman candle,
        Independence Day night-length.

Scattering like so much seed-corn
    Back-truck M-80's are borne—
        Flung out to the sky, far and wide.
Sparklers, snakes and Chinese dragons
    A kind of strip tease coronation
        For glory days and pride.

Pride—that explodes with our pop culture
    Into the blind, loaded future
        Their heart's delight and recreation.
Older people who stay indoors
    Mind their stores, keep baseball scores
        —Or take a long vacation.

Enter The Circle

She is more than a prideful child
With her tantrums and demands,
You've got to grow to reach her,
For her to want to take your hand.
Follow where she leads you
When she takes you to a place
Where you cannot recognize your features,
Where you and strange creatures come face to face.

Is a strange brew boys and girls,
Better than diamonds, better than pearls,
For the moon in all her phases
        Enter the circle.

A warrior bids you take a sword,
A veiled woman offers you a purple cup,
The hangman stands at his gallows,
He wants to string you up.
The tax collector is knocking on your door
Pounding with some poor boy's skull,
Silver bells are ringing in the village,
Is your cup half empty or half full?

Is a strange brew boys and girls,
Better than diamonds, better than pearls,
For the moon in all her phases
        Enter the circle.

No one rents the trees and stars,
A prince who loves the mighty night
Believes in the Queen of Hearts,
Who hides her heart and hides her light.
A blind man shakes a cup in his face,
A one-armed man throws some stones,
To be about the heaven's work,
The guards throw their dogs some bones.

Is a strange brew boys and girls,
Better than diamonds, better than pearls,
For the moon in all her phases
    Enter the circle.

Dreamer's Bottom

As punishment for his gay liaisons
The Czar offers public exposure or poison,
Did he catch cholera or down arsenic
Aborting the glory of his music?

Chorus

> Be my Alabama chicken.
> > I'll be your Georgia lamb.
> And we can dine together
> Down in Hunger-land.

The gospel girls got relief from boredom,
Salem's Tituba taught voodoo whoredom.
When Paris caught them naked in the woods,
To save themselves they blamed the neighborhood.

Chorus

> Be my Alabama chicken.
> > I'll be your Georgia lamb.
> And we can dine together
> Down in Hunger-land.

What The Bluebird Said

Before the day is dead
Listen to what
The bluebird said
    to me,
'In another place
The sunshine is a face
Too bright
    to see.'

The Fifties

Leave It To Beaver, Father Knows Best,
Twilight Zone and *Howdy Doody*,
Waiting 'til recess—rough play by
      the jungle gym,
The Sputnik is first in space! Will the Soviets
      bomb us from the moon?
The Cuban missile crisis, air-raid drills,
Long snowy lines of commuters, waiting for the school bus,
That big white soccer ball kept turning over
      and over,
I could see the seams so perfectly,
As I made my headlong dive.

We would chug beer down like meisters
During our weekly card games talk of girls,
If only Heather's parents would go away
      for the weekend,
If only Diane was not a prude,
Before time did what time does to us pilgrims,
As we weave our path to Wall St. or out by the abandoned
      highways, or a tour of duty in Vietnam.

I heard the story of Joseph's coat of many colors—
How the dreamer was thrown into a pit,
Taken off with a caravan to a foreign land,
How he rose through the ranks and became a king's favorite
Because he was wise with dreams.
'Remember your dreams,' my great-uncle would say.

My father, who rarely left his neighborhood
      in Brooklyn, surrounded as he was by
         wild Irish, Latino, black,
My father who adored classical music
      and looked down on Glenn Miller,
Who served in the Navy following
      World War 2, and learned about radars
        and rubbers,
He worked 12 hours a day, I rarely saw him,
Dr. Know (or No) he called himself,
While talking about Do-loops and deadlines,
      indifferent to baseball, football,
        a brilliant man, my father.
If only Heather's parents would go away,
If only Diane was not a prude...

The Swimmer

He stands, at dawn, by lake's edge,
In clear, crystal water he sees
An oval, soft, unbroken and clear
Certain of all that breathes,
And certain of all that is still,
Moon set like a jewel in the night,
Sun to its circuits kept,
Like a watch wound tight.

The lake, as smooth as a lady's glass,
He enters, enters in
To lovers' lives or solitary hours,
The images begin
To shiver sweetly in their shape,
Lose their bottom from their top,
Lose their simple certainty,
Forever, and forever crack.
The mirror splinters and flies,
Lights through a thousand skies.

Devotion

Devotion, more than loving,
    Less captive to chance,
A mother with her child,
Has armor against circumstance.

Sometimes in action humble
As a beggar wearing rags,
A quiet victory is sweet
And need not wave a flag.

Superior of design
As a boy or girl,
Emotion, not to be sounded,
On the bottom is a pearl.

Devotion, like a hummingbird,
A balance from the breast,
Until the flower is disclosed,
The nectar in the nest.

Late Afternoon Walk

Up the broad avenues
Of the pastel city
The harried minstrel walks,
His mind on eternity
Passing the friendly schoolgirls
And busy shoppers—
He eats strawberries
At a Chinatown stand
And builds up the clouds above
With passing references to camels.
Then twilight bleeds over his favorite cathedral.
Rimbaud shoved his hands in his pockets
And went to Africa,
A slave-trader abandoning something
—Nights pregnant with 1000 explosions,
China's and Brooklyn's lighting the waterfronts,
Virile tenderness of future architectures
And the men and women who will raise them,
Palaces floating on the sea.

After Bruegel

A castle is burning across the waters,
And through the air creatures softly glide
In their blue dirigibles.

A pillar of smoke drifts over the waters,
Three men fight over a piece of bread,
A man whips a boy with a quartz rock on his back,
Two girls fight off a man, beating him with fish heads.

A man is drowning in quicksand,
Only his head and his hands are visible,
   clawing the air,
A farmer thrashes his pig,
And a woman carries off a sack of wheat.

Two children jump in a hole in the ground
And shiver with fear
As three men pass over their heads
   on a little wooden bridge
     beating and cursing their donkey.

2

Penumbra

for L.

He trips in the narrow hall
And opens the heavy wooden door.
The suburban night is rich with stars.
He cannot remember why he is here,
    the beheaded dreamer.

He got layed off last week.
A Ford Ranger barrels down the street.
He lays the dead leaves on the curb
And turns away from the trash bag,
    the beheaded dreamer.

A dog is barking not far away.
His neighbor's patio is almost done.
He hears laughter in their rose garden,
He forgets what he came here for,
    the beheaded dreamer.

The Jack Of Hearts

'every saint has a past, every sinner has a future.'

Here I am a messenger on the lam,
Having half forgotten the message,
And my horse gallops so fast,
And the countryside is so breathtaking
That there is a chance I have overridden the war,
Paul Revere in limbo.
Will we ever graduate, and go on to the next level,
Some kind of a grand union
With a divine inflow?
My reputation has been turned topsy-turvy
     by the baron of conformal symmetries,
        and the dutchess of earl.

If...

If your ears should desert you,
I would be your ears.
If your mouth should go away,
I would open
I would be your mouth.
If your eyes should be sewn shut
I would find my way to you,
I would be your eyes.
Because you are in the treetops,
Rock me in the boughs,
Your soft breathing breast,
Rhythm of the ages,
Sunny woman.
Because wherever you go there is a perfume,
A soft scent and a sea breeze,
Beauty walks and with delight.
Child and mother, source of nourishment,
Reaching, ever-reaching,
As a magician dissolves to the evening
And takes his light to bed.
These the ceremonies of innocence,
These the healing zephyrs,
This earth and sky, red-grey field at twilight.
Another by our side, much greater
If we are aware, profers a hand,
Extends a hand and helps us across.

Dyin' Into The Night

The kids
walk away.

The man
with his dog
walks away.

The traffic eases.
'The traffic lights turn blue tomorrow.'

Peets closes, off go the lights.

Haven't picked up
a pen like this
in a couple of months.
What difference does it make?

Mother with baby
    snoozin' in baby carriage
baby just starting out,
I dyin' into the night.

3

Devotional

Jesus, Buddha, Shakespeare three men of the same
    divine spirit,
Develop faculties of mind and soul harmoniously,
After growing into one's gifts help others,
Shed light and heat for others,
Repentance and forgiveness
    a kind of zenith,
Pardon all,
Be an angel of the world, for your own sake,
Or a short sighted selfish animal,
Be a cup bearer undying,
Soul is wine.

$500...$400...$300...$100?
I will not get paid for this poem.
Christ, Keats, Whitman rarely get paid,
Nor Emily Dickinson, or Hart Crane.
Jack London gets paid well, and spends it on
    extravagant adventures, outfitting his ship Snark,
        and sailing the Pacific, springing leaks, audacious Quixote.

"Skeletons play the harmonica keys in the rain..."

Does the light come after the darkness,
Will the woman soul be waiting,
Who knows, who can tell?
Each man, Browning says,
With two soul sides,
One to show the world,
One to show the woman he loves,
Great doer,
Stir the sentient air,
In a great ceremony.

Rodin's regret,
A dozen types all swallowed up and lost
In the vague womb of uncreated night,
Til one loves a man, a woman
One cannot understand them.

The heart of the battle is
Have you done your work?
Death is the seal,
The work is there,
A final judgment.

Prometheus is the rebel who defies Jove,
    brings fire to man,
And similarly man must sometimes rebel
Against conditions that would dwarf him,

And hinder the growth of his bright
   clear light,
The heart of the rose.
Be courageous and warlike,
Be kind-hearted and a peacemaker,
Anointed with a spirit of independence,
Also possessed of reverence and regard
   for order,
Be a doubter and have faith,
Hand down a legacy, unafraid of beauty,
We decay in time
But time is eternal.

Untouchables

Dim dark moon,
Shuttered rooms,
Savage footsteps,
The thug with a knife creeps up on the
   honest man with his back turned
   while he is making supper,
But this man has a shotgun and backs
   the thug out the door,
But a machine gun pierces the night
And the honest man goes down,
He dies in his doorway on the mean streets,
Overpowering opera on the radio
As two thugs make their getaway in a Mercedes.

Abandoned Child

A little girl tiptoed into her mother's room
    once, not long ago, remember,
      carrying some fresh baked sweets from the kitchen,
        and happy hours at the stove...
Ah, but the orphanages are not so concerned
    as a mother.
Someone's turned on the Rain Machine.
You told me tales of jails and assaults,
      tales of the caged bird and the lures and jesses,
        how they framed you for everything
          under the sun, threw you down
      and left you to die
        under black clouds in the rain,
'cause of what happened by a car,
'cause of what happened in a field,
      that started it all, and gave you thunder
        in your head, migraines,
          whose cure is wine...

The Blizzard of 2012

Tom Snowman, Lou Daybreak, Siberia Sally
—I'd go out twice a day with my trusty broom
   as snow piled up on my Mercury Tracer
     and with big, sweeping motions
        start dusting.
—The entire town was snowed in Thursday to Sunday.
—Accumulation a couple of feet and worse than that
   severe, imposing ice storms that welded shut
     car doors and froze fuel lines
       —leaving us incarcerated, squelched.
That is how I met them,
   they helped me shovel out,
     and I was glad to return the favor.
After a session in the deep freeze,
     cursing and puffing,
   we would go over to the little Italian deli
     our last outpost, and we would gobble up
       turkey roll, and meatball heros, talking tough
      about the weather, while poor, shivering
         mongrels barked by the door,
    begging for scraps.

Notes

1. *Scenes From Law School.* I passed the Bar in
1984, and tried my hand at criminal law, patent,
trademark and copyright law, landlord tenant law, and
constitutional law. It was over pretty fast. I ended up
co-managing a music club for a few years in upstate
New York, and eventually taught high school English.

2. *Swan Island.* A poem to my father. Miss you Dad,
rest in peace.

3. "The Weaver And The Shepherd" is based on a story
in *The Crimson Fairy Book.*

Made in the USA
Columbia, SC
08 January 2024

30095395R10048